Autobiography

DAVID SPENCER

Copyright © 2020 by David Spencer
ISBN: Paperback   978-1-951670-20-7
              eBook   978-1-951670-21-4

All rights reserved. No part of this publication may be reproduced, distributed, or transmitted in any form or by any electronic or mechanical means, without the prior written permission of the publisher, except in the case of brief quotations embodied in critical reviews and certain other noncommercial uses permitted by copyright law.

Ordering Information:
For orders and inquiries, please contact:
books@authorsnote360.com
www.authorsnote360.com

Printed in the United States of America

For Marilyn

"I recognized
Your words at once
They feel
What I have always felt,
But never could express"

Acknowledgement

Writing a book is a journey. It needs imagination, motivation and of course passion. Publishing my books will not be realized without the support of the people around me.

I'd like to start with Emma Reading (My Wife's Mother) for all the compliments and words of encouragement she has given me. Her words served as my guide to the right direction in writing.

To my very good friends Sam Wilson and Jeff Yelton for all the support they have shown and for pushing me to work on my book.

To our family friends:

- Sandy and Fred Hardy
- Tim and Carol Dionne

Our family is so blessed to have a family friend like you. Always remember that you are always dear to our family.

To my Publisher Author's Note 360, I thank you for showing interest and for believing in my book. I thank the whole team for making this republication possible.

Finally, I dedicate this book to my beautiful and ever supportive wife Marilyn Spencer, the LOVE OF MY LIFE. She's been a huge fan of my books and she supported me all the way. She stood by me in sickness and in health. She's always been the source of my strength and my inspiration. Without her, I'm not sure if I'd be able to finish even a single book. To my beloved Marilyn, I thank you and I love you so much.

Heritage

By David Spencer

She says I have my Father's hands,
peasant brown leather,
large veined, thin fingered.
Delicate, they might have played piano…
hands translating Russian soldiers,
Polish refugees,
stood guard at the gate
of a south Chicago Steel Mill
gave their lines, their folds to me.
Loving, as they held my Mother,
not so, as he left her…
hands that flew in an Iowa courtroom
drove down roads, and roads through limestone -
farms, and farms, and farms.
Frail and crippled, they embraced me -
years, and years, and years had passed…
now they have become my hands,
loving, as I hold my Wife,
loving, as I live my life.

Slavic Easter

By David Spencer

In the shape of a Cross on the wall,
leaves from the palms of Palm Sunday
are nailed, as if to ward off spirits…
baskets of food to Easter Mass,
like offerings to a temple.
The procession bends down,
at the end of the mass
to kiss the wound
in the side of the Crucifix.

Starlight on Snowdrifts

By David Spencer

(a Federal housing project in Gary, 1960)
The cold has seeped in,
through red brick walls -
gray concrete floors have grown colder…
the coal burning metal stove's
gone colder too,
as ghosts of our Christmas Songs
huddle for warmth…
soon, "The First of The Month"
will be here,
with money for food,
to turn the lights back on
and the Star of Bethlehem
sparkles on snowdrifts,
reflecting the tinsel,
our small brittle tree…
and I dream of the box
with the "snow man" tag
and the gift someone's giving to me.

Country Road

By David Spencer

A horizon of dried grass
flowing like wheat,
waved with the wind in the blue sky,
bright sun…
fenced in fields of rows of flowers
lined the Country Road.
Sun dried earth, and sun dried dust
curled past the blackberry bush,
hickory tree, grape vine…
curved 'til completed, a dusty circle
we called the Country Road.
Sunset came cool in the Summer evening…
moist air, warm Summer rain
might form a rainbow.
Walking back home
with our "arrow- heads", slowly,
back down our Country Road.

The Mountains of Man

By David Spencer

The mountains rise up,
from the south western desert :
gray, and blue, and huge in the distance…
mountains,
the home of ancient cliff-dwellers
seal the remains in layers of rock.
The mountains encircle the aging barracks,
stronghold
against ghosts of vengeful Apache,
camped in the hills, in primitive hatred
high in the Mountains of Man.
Echoes of ancestors, hunting with stone tools
blend with the echoes of cavalry charges,
blend with the sand and heat of the desert
there in the Mountains of Man.

The Spirit of the Bayonet
By David Spencer

An August night, the moon's blood red :
red "tracer" bullets overhead…
"don't stand up," they told us;
"what's the spirit of the bayonet?"
"to kill, drill sergeant."
Explosive charges left and right,
crawl under barbed wire in the night—
"what's the spirit of the bayonet?"
"to kill, kill, drill sergeant."
More dynamite charges, rocks and logs,
more "tracer" bullets split the night…
the "tracers" - glowing, deadly, beckoning,
contrast the black sky, and bright stars;
"don't stand up," they told us -
i wanna be an airborne ranger,
i wanna live a life of danger
i wanna go to viet nam,
i wanna kill the charlie cong
"What's the spirit of the bayonet?"…
to kill, kill, kill, drill sergeant.

The Crime

By David Spencer

A broken man was plodding through the snow,
the alleys' snow
that turns to slush in spring…
frozen fingers clutched a loaf of bread,
a ragged trouser leg was stiff with blood.
He made his way through trash cans,
tires, fences
crawled to a shabby lean to in the mud…
The frozen train cars,
rusted, filled with snow…
a frozen fortress for the frozen dead.

Boy on a Pony
By David Spencer

When South Chicago
was still a Polish Village,
as the ancient scissors sharpener
wheels his grindstone down the street,
as the bearded scissors sharpener
wheels his grindstone down the street…
a compulsory ritual, almost ceremonial
like posing for a portrait,
like the offspring of royalty…
a five year old, squinting in the sun
smiling a child's smile, mounted on a pony
a brown and white pony, half asleep
staring dumbly into oblivion.
A cowboy hat, and a faded red kerchief
worn by dozens of five-year-olds
as the ancient scissors sharpener
wheels his grindstone down the street,
as the bearded scissors sharpener
wheels his grindstone down the street.

In the Shadow of the Skyway

By David Spencer

In the shadow of the Skyway,
distant memories hang on :
of sunny days, rainy days, ancient days—
days of misty rays of sunlight
filtering through clouds
of steel-mill smoke…
past masses, traditions, holiday meals,
people long ago forgotten, moved away,
left behind…
Now, that world exists in memories,
lives on only in the mind;
When those who lived in the South Side
in the 40's, 50's, 60's are all gone
the South Chicago Skyway
will be just a bridge for traffic,
nothing in the past, nothing beyond.

In Snowy Meadows

By David Spencer

In Snowy Meadows
misty woods
the seedlings sleep
beneath the snow…
the sparrows
perched on frozen branches
wait to see the seedlings grow…
The flowers live
That we may live…
they push their way
up through the snow,
The sparrows
perched on blossomed branches
sing to see the flowers grow.

Polish Village

By David Spencer

(South Chicago, 1953)
The warm summer night - trees shining,
rustling gently in the streetlight…
And the Steel Mill, always the Mill—
looming large, a gray metal mountain
blocking out the sun.
The flashing neon bubbles, floating,
rising from the champagne glass
in the window of the bar on the corner…
just lying on a bed on a hot summer night,
staring blankly at the reflection
of the ceiling light in the window,
or the moth fluttering near the light,
or the pattern of the bricks
of the house crowded next door.
And the Steel Mill, always the Mill—
looming large, a gray metal mountain
blocking out the sun.

Uncle Tony

By David Spencer

Eighty years old, and danced the polka...
the retired mill guard
sat watching wrestling from Milwaukee
with his can of "Old Style",
alone in his room on East 79th Place,
across the Illinois Central tracks,
near Uncle Johnny the crane operator,
and Uncle Eddie the mill guard,
and Uncle Chester the Goldblatt's butcher...
a few blocks from St. Michael's,
a medieval castle
towering over a peasant village...
Eighty years old, and danced the polka
my Great Uncle Tony.

South Chicago

By David Spencer

Tall brick buildings,
with attics and basements,
brown brick buildings, built in the 30s
surround the god, "Steel Mill",
engulf the church, St Michael's Cathedral,
towering like a medieval castle
over a peasant village.
South shore tracks of the Illinois Central,
olive drab metal, tan rattan seats
clunking, jolting through South Chicago
83rd Street to Roosevelt Road,
steep zig-zag wooden stairs
blackened with age.
Get up in the morning, work in the Mill,
go home when you're through,
or go to the tavern.
Get up in the morning, work in the Mill,
rise and kneel in the Church on Sunday.

Bessie

By David Spencer

Her hair was still dark in the fifties, perhaps with flecks of gray
like the fur coat she wore that autumn nineteen - fifties style.
She came to our house in Chicago, and stood inside the doorway.
I remember her reflection in the long door-mirror,
as she stood in the doorway, laughing.
When I asked, "What's the matter, Grandma?"
she may have glanced down for a moment.
Then Bessie became John Wayne movies, cigarettes,
"Family Feud", crossword puzzles, Zane Grey novels…
and always a spoonful of "Real-Lemon" juice
in a glass of cool August iced tea.
The end, when it cam was expected.
Expected, yet somehow unreal, impossible…
When I stood at her grave-site that summer,
It was not like a grave at all
Just a dried-out square of yellow grass
bordered by dry clods of earth.
A spot for a small bronze plaque, memorial flowers…
and all I could think of was, "Real-Lemon" juice
in a glass of cool August iced tea.

Abandoned

By David Spencer

A dried out, weed grown, dusty path
through a dense, primeval jungle
dragonflies, mosquitoes
hover over a steaming, stagnant trickle
like prehistoric insects
over an algae-covered pond.
In an abandoned auditorium,
rows and rows of folding chairs,
the green metal Army-style folding chairs
are seen through the thick, aging
blocks of window - glass of the fifties.
A tall, thin metal microphone
on an aging wooden platform
leads the rows of dusty metal chairs
in a silent prayer to the god of the fifties.

Metamorphosis
By David Spencer

A tree
becomes a thin white birch tree
smooth bark shining,
dry leaves glistening
fluttering in an autumn breeze
in the bright September morning sun.
The call of a bird
becomes the cry of the wild birds,
soaring in the forest sky
and the sunset
becomes the glow of sunset
rising up behind mountains of clouds,
billowing up,
behind the leafless winter woods.

Dells, 1954

By David Spencer

The Sauk Fox dance the tribal dance, for descendents
of those who have conquered…
through rocky, wooded waterways,
through ghosts of the Sauk - Fox canoes,
amphibious crafts guide the tourists,
descendents of those who have conquered.
The forests, the cliffs and the valleys
succumb to the god, "Souvenir"…
the spirits of trees,
of earth, air and water
give way to the god, "Motel"…
the god of the primitive T.V. set,
crackling colorless re-runs of, "Amos n' Andy"…
the god of the Labor- Day traveler, "Motel"

"Pale Eyes"
By David Spencer

There is a pale glow,
in the eyes of the dying...
a far away, dull look
of fear, then surrender
waiting... hopeless...
like corral on a reef,
like barnacles on a hull,
clinging grimly to remnants of life,
drifting steadily downward,
waiting...

Photosynthesis

By David Spencer

He took in the sunlight
at dawn, with a clear sky,
at sunset, through clouds;
He took in the world,
and breathed out perceptions…
inspiration grew higher, higher,
reaching for the sun.
He gathered the rays of light
into his cells,
breathing out words in verse,
all with "deep meaning"…
and in the dark,
there he remained :
neck craning, straining,
toward where the sun had been.

Hank's Song

By David Spencer

Keep house for me, Trudy
in a small town in Iowa,
as I leave my wife in anger
in a small town in Indiana,
as I leave my three small children
alone in a small town in Indiana…
as I take down words, and words,
in an Iowa courtroom.
My family, my old job, my old life
are far away, in Chicago.
Keep house for me, Trudy
and share my loneliness…
share my pain too, for I am ill…
Stay with me for eternity, Trudy
as I lie on a hilltop
near the dust and gravel
of a roadside in Iowa,
as herds of wild deer
charge across the snow covered fields…
stay with me forever.

Reunion, 1970

By David Spencer

I wrote to you, from an Army Post in Kansas.
You lived in Iowa, with your 2nd wife.
I wrote to you, from an Army Post in Kansas.
I said, "15 years is a long time"… it was.
You wrote to me, from your home in Iowa.
You told me that you would drive down.
A barracks friend said, "I'm happy for you, Ski."
You wrote to me, from your home in Iowa.
A One-day "reunion", then back to Iowa to stay.
And now… 42 years is a long time for you to be gone.
I've visited your grave in Iowa, Dad.

Jogging into Memory – 1978
By David Spencer

Like a satellite,
circling in orbit
the runner circles the track…
and to counter the weariness, boredom
stares at the track as he runs,
at the track moving by as he runs.
And his mind, turning into a blank
drifts to running the mile in school,
drifts to running the mile in "Basic"…
The mile is the same,
and the track is the same,
as the runner jogs on, into memory.

Moments in Memory, 1953
By David Spencer

Imagination, stories were the world
combined with church, and school, and relatives.
Fireworks on a moonlit summer shore,
witches burned in effigy in autumn.
Old World food, and speech, and customs
Old world music, dreams, and people.
Exploratory walks, alone.
A black straw witch, perched on a broomstick,
hurled into the fire with shout,
burned to ashes with a cheer
and the child, dressed up as a pirate,
rouge and a bandana
the child stands silently, watching
etching the moment in memory.

Ancestry

By David Spencer

The heart beats, the blood flows…
life is given, the child grows.
The moon, and constellations of the stars
are seen through pupils, retinas,
strong hands grasp iron bars.
The silent male
is filled with silent rage…
metallic etchings
form the word "Gorilla" on the cage.

Pro Deo et Patria

By David Spencer

Weatherworn names,
carved on the monument
stone resting there,
like an ancient ruin.
The broken stone steps
are crowned with a garland:
the jagged green glass
of the broken wine bottles.
"Pro Deo et Patria - For god and Country"
lists the soldiers who made
the "East - Side Honor Roll."

An Alley In Gary
By David Spencer

The streetlight in the alley
shines on leafless branches,
on the kind of trees
that grow on sand dunes,
like a searchlight, in a prison compound…
the aging house behind the fence
looks like a sagging,
white-washed Baptist Church,
somewhere in Appalachia.
The aging picket fence
should be in some neglected
country grave-yard,
with crumbling grave-stones
peering out,
behind the missing slats.

Tribute

By David Spencer

One of the many,
his ancient past was not revealed to us…
One of the many,
his story was not told.
They said he was a derelict,
a bum from off the road.
He might have fallen, bloody,
in some un-named, forgotten battlefield.
He might have drowned, helpless,
in some sunken, hulking wreck,
among the barnacles,
among the coral reefs,
in some distant, un-named sea.
Instead, he's here in our homeland,
in our earth,
in our town ;
Today, we meet to honor him
no longer is he "unknown".

Algonquin Summer
By David Spencer

An aroma of Autumn flows through the air,
like aged "tabac"
curling up from an old pipe,
a brown, mellow meerschaum,
or polished briar,
smoked by the warmth of a fire in Autumn… Shades of light,
warm spots in the cool wind,
a walk in the woods,
with the shades of Autumn…
A day for the dead, a day for All Saints
Cold, grey rain from the skies of October,
clear, mild days of "Algonquin Summer".

Eastern European Photograph
(Great-Grand Parents in Poland, 1959)

By David Spencer

They are posed, in the cavernous doorway
of a picturesque old wooden dwelling,
like a scene
from the heart of the German Black Forest,
the Gingerbread House of Hansel & Gretel.
His leathery peasant hands,
long and bony with age,
are like his bony wooden cane,
dried out and hardened by time…
her wizened peasant face,
sunken and wrinkled with age…
hand folded, eyes hooded
stares coldly ahead,
into a cold camera lens.
Dressed in simple peasant clothes,
their simple peasant shoes
are planted on their peasants' porch,
on photographic paper.

History – Fiction
By David Spencer

The Sound was barely audible,
like the gentle noise
made by the metal horse-trappings
as the muscles of the animals
lurched slowly forward
with the movement of their hooves.
In late autumn,
the tall feather - grass of the Steppes
was dried out,
giving way to the hooves unwillingly…
The Nomad Saka Cavalry
came upon a huge burial kurgan,
a mound of earth worn away by time.

The Kurgan

By David Spencer

The top layer of the earthen mound
had been blown away
by the wind of the Steppes,
exposing the death-guard
of a fallen Saka king.
The riders who were still erect
sat upon the saddled bones
of their horses…
tattered remnants of clothing
that still clung to the bodies
of the death-guard fluttered in the wind.
Small silver bells hung from their horses,
from the worn leather death-masks
of their mounts…
as the bells moved with the wind,
they played a hollow, haunting tune.

Steppe Clans
By David Spencer

Dawn on the northern shore,
on the ancient shore of the Black Sea.
Tent-Nomads take their herds to pasture,
as a flowing sea of Nomad Horse-Bowmen
rides the flowing Steppe-lands.
In the royal tent of the Nomad Chieftain,
enemy skulls filled with molten gold
rest on the colorful carpet,
on the red and gold woven carpet
decorated with royal Golden Stags.
The Chieftain's horse, a small Mongol pony
has enemy scalps, hanging from its bridle.
The Nomad god of the sun, Oetosyrus
gleams in the dawn from the royal shield,
gleams in the dawn from the sacred Golden Stag.
Dusk on the northern shore,
on the ancient shore of the Black Sea.
The Nomads, a flowing sea of ox-drawn house-wagons,
of black felt tents, vanish
in the frozen sea of time.

The Lamassu

By David Szpejnowski /Spencer

At those Royal gates of Nineveh,
I stood as though transfixed;
spellbound looking up, ever higher
to the great stone statues
of the sacred Winged Bulls, the Lamassi
The winged Lamassu had long muscular legs,
the hooves of bulls, the paws of lions
like powerful animals in their stride.
The great stone wings made the gods look
as though they were in flight,
like some kind of giant eagles.
High above the wings, the rock hard gods
wore the tall Royal Assyrian crowns.
The winged gods
had the faces of the kings of Ashur…
the long, stony beards combined
the strength of the bulls and the lions
with the deity
of the Royal House of Assyria.

The Sarmatian

By David Spencer

In the days of time forgotten
we rode from the Caspian plains,
to the northern shore of the Black Sea.
In the misty days of our distant past,
we rode against them…
we lost to Pompey the Great then,
66 years before the Christ.
In the time of our fore-fathers,
our kinsmen rode against them again…
they were defeated at Zela then,
by their General Julius Caesar,
47 years before the Christ.
I am Perun, a horseman of the Alani,
named after our god of thunder…
I ride south across the Danube,
to meet with our allies the Goths,
to ride against their Emperor Valens.
toward the battle-ground at Adrianople.

The Drekkar

By David Spencer

Through the North Atlantic,
Drekkar, Dragon- ships
push their way straight through the sea
Through the North Atlantic Drekkar, Dragon ships
carry men who are wild and strong and free.
Men who pray to Odin, Loki and to Thor
leave their misty home-land for a distant shore.
Through the North Atlantic,
Drekkar, Dragon- ships
push their way straight through the sea
Through the North Atlantic Drekkar, Dragon ships
carry men who are wild and strong and free.
Men who seek Valhalla, battle-axe in hand
sail uncharted waters toward a distant land.
Through the North Atlantic,
Drekkar, Dragon- ships
push their way straight through the sea
Through the North Atlantic Drekkar, Dragon ships
carry men who are wild and strong and free.

A Pagan Death

By David Spencer

The wind from the North Sea shook the beams
of thatched roofs, old and strong…
the sea rose up, came down in waves
with a force that rocked the shore…
A Viking sword slashed through the waves,
slashed through the icy rain…
a helmet, and determined will,
against the icy pain.
The morning sun was glowing, warm…
cool waves lapped gently up on shore…
The Christian Norsemen found him then,
A Pagan, fallen there to Thor.

Stone Elk

By David Spencer

In the dawn of time,
when the world was new,
when the hills were green
and the waters blue…
Warrior Stone Elk
in the mist of dawn,
running through the clouds
that have come to rest.
Rays of sun shine through,
like the crown of God…
and cloud-dancing birds
hover in the blue.
At the end of day,
far into the West
see the sun, pulled down
by the hand of God.
Misty light of moon,
shining in the clouds;
Stone Elk is at rest,
in the Earth's dark shroud.

Krakowiak

By David Spencer

You lie in state, Il Papa
like Lenin
in his Muscovite Tomb.
They have placed you
in your robe and crown,
lying beneath a Crucifix.
Cardinals
locked up in the Vatican
cast their ballots…
reporters and their cameras
circle about you, in a sort of
"Dance Macabre."
In the grotto
of St. Peter's Basilica
you will rest,
Karol Wojtyla of Krakow.

Dreams of Irish Songs
by David Spencer

*"I wish I was in Carrickfergus,
only for nights in Ballygrand…"*

Around St. Patrick's Day,
I would start singing "Clancy Brothers" tunes to myself,
as I walked down the street in the bright March sunshine
on my way to work,
as I walked down the street in the cold March winds,
on my way to the store.

*"Oh, then tell me, Sean O' Farrell, tell me why you
hurry so?…"*

That year as I lay in a hospital bed, -
tubes, morphine, blood tests -
I wasn't free to sing, *"Kelly the boy from Killan"*,
Or, *"One Sunday mornin', while on the way to Mass."*
I missed the freedom of it; I missed being outside.

All I was free to do was look out the window,
thinking, "I'll be out of here soon."
I was in "solitary" waiting for a pardon.
On St. Patrick's Day, the hospital tray
had "shamrock" napkins - it made me feel low.
There wasn't any humming of, *"Whiskey's in the jar- o."*
"I'll be out of here soon" - days later, I was.
So, my next St. Patrick's Day promise to myself
was to walk somewhere in the bright March sunshine,
to walk somewhere in the cold March winds, singing,
"...for the pikes must be together, by the risin' of the moon."
- a song of freedom for the free.